Invitation to a PARTY

Lillenas Drama

Invitation to a PARTY

And Other Scripts for Children

by
Debbie Salter Goodwin

Lillenas PUBLISHING COMPANY

KANSAS CITY, MO 64141

10 9 8 7 6 5 4 3 2 1

Dedicated to
my father
Marlow "Salty" Salter
who is already enjoying the Party
that these scripts celebrate.
And
with grateful appreciation to
Judi Amerson
and the children's camps she directed
where these scripts
were born, rehearsed, and premiered.

Contents

About the Invitation

Everybody loves a party. Especially children. Since Jesus said heaven will be like one big party, maybe we need to start rehearsing now. Who can teach us better than children that the essence of abundant life is celebration.

That's where these plays come in. They feature the parables Jesus used to help all of us understand what the kingdom of heaven is all about and the meaning of abundant life on earth.

The plays included in this collection are easy to rehearse. They require two to three one-hour rehearsals. There is little or no memorization work. Most, if not all, the preparation required for performing each script can be completed during rehearsals. Rehearsals could be a part of another children's activity such as Sunday School, children's church, Vacation Bible School, or a weekday kids' club.

Following each script is a rehearsal plan implementing creative dramatic strategies explained in the book *Just for the Play of It*. The rehearsal plan divides rehearsal time into three parts: Getting into the Act, Acting It Out, and Taking the Act Home.

Getting into the Act engages children in preparatory activities that will establish a creative and affirming atmosphere. Warm-up activities introduce group acting, which is a prerequisite to handing out parts in the next section. All exercises point toward the message and/or activities from the play.

After warm-up activities, the group should be ready to start Acting It Out. This section introduces the actual rehearsal of the script and always starts with a review of the scripture on which the play is based. Follow instructions carefully concerning when to hand out written scripts. Introducing scripts too early will block creative thinking and acting. Without a script in hand, children will move and express with more freedom.

Reserve 10 minutes at the end of your rehearsal for discussion with your young actors. Ask simple questions concerning what the play means to them and what they want an audience to remember. When the children generate a key idea based on what they have been rehearsing, you can be sure they are going to be Taking the Act Home.

Remember, you've been invited to a party. Every rehearsal and performance should reflect this truth. Since children know best how to celebrate, let them find their voice through these plays and teach us what we have nearly forgotten.

1

INVITATION TO A PARTY

(Luke 14:16-24)

Characters:

NARRATOR: *an adult, teen, or expressive reader*
HOST: *rich but not overly impressed with wealth*
2 (or more) SERVANTS
2 (or more) DECORATING CREW (could be the servants)
GUEST 1: *a farmer*
GUEST 2: *a cowboy or cowgirl*
GUEST 3: *a harried father or mother*
3 (or more) STREET PEOPLE

Costumes:

HOST dressed in modern clothes, indicating wealth.
SERVANTS wear white shirts or blouses with black slacks or skirts. Girls can add white aprons.
GUEST 1 in clothes like jeans, T-shirt, and bandanna.
GUEST 2 wears cowboy clothes: boots, red bandanna, and cowboy hat.
GUEST 3 dressed in baseball T-shirt and cap and carries ball glove.
STREET PEOPLE wear torn and dirty clothes and carry bags.

Props:

Small table and chair
Box appearing to be filled with invitations
4 invitations
Party decorations ready for quick decorating. Example: balloons already blown up with streamers attached. Keep in mind that servants must be able to bring all decorations in one trip and attach in one action. An alternative is to decorate a portable chalkboard and simply roll it in.
Brightly colored party table cloth
Party centerpiece: Decorative gift bag overflowing with tissue paper and curled ribbon. May also add balloons.
Any kind of food indicating a party: chips, cookies, cans of soda, empty pizza boxes, etc.

Stage Arrangement:

Table is center stage. Chair is angled at left center. NARRATOR enters to stand down right throughout play, out of the way of other action. HOST enters to stand center stage in front of table. He holds his head high and takes long, strutting steps. While speaking, he uses his arms to gesture expansively.

HOST:
> I want to throw a party.
> I feel I'm in the mood.
> I want a lot of people.
> I want a lot of food.

(SERVANTS *enter. They stand in front of* HOST *on either side, bodies slightly turned toward audience while still facing* HOST. HOST *stops pacing to stand in front of the table.* HOST *gives orders, pointing alternately to each servant. As soon as* SERVANT *receives instructions,* SERVANT *exits the same way he entered.*)

NARRATOR:
> He ordered all his servants;
> Gave each a job to do;
> To clean and bake and organize
> And then he hired a crew . . .

(DECORATING CREW *enters stage left. Working left to right, they attach balloons, spread tablecloth, and place centerpiece.*)

NARRATOR:
> To decorate the banquet hall
> With balloons and ribbons bright,
> And streamers hung from wall to wall.
> It was a colorful sight.

(HOST *looks around pleased and dismisses* DECORATING CREW. SERVANT *enters stage left carrying a box of invitations.*)

NARRATOR:
> He ordered invitations made
> And with these words, expressed:

(SERVANT *crosses to* HOST *and shows* HOST *invitation.*)

HOST *(reading):*
> "I'm going to have a party.
> Would you come be my guest?
> It's going to be on Friday
> With food and fun for all.
> You'll make me very happy
> If you come, one and all."

(HOST *sits at table and begins to sign invitations.* SERVANT *seals and stamps at least one using big, exaggerated gestures.* HOST *gives box to* SERVANT, *who exits stage left as if to mail them.* HOST *looks around, nods head with pleasure, and exits stage left.*)

NARRATOR: He signed and sealed and stamped them.
                  He sent them off by mail.
             Now everything was ready.
                  His party could not fail.

(GUESTS 1, 2, *and* 3 *enter stage right and take downstage places with appropriate space between them. Each has an invitation to open and read. Each shakes head, indicating rejection of the invitation. Each* GUEST *takes a freeze pose when not speaking.*)

NARRATOR: But as the invitations
                  Arrived, guests shook their heads.
             They each made sorry gestures
                  And sent regrets instead.

GUEST 1:   I can't go next Friday.
                  I've bought a brand-new field.
             I've got to plow and seed it.
                  I have no time to yield.

GUEST 2:   I've got no time to party.
                  I've bought a brand-new herd.
             They must be watered, fed, and penned.
                  To leave them is absurd!

GUEST 3:   You want *me* at a party?
                  But I'm a family man.
             Soccer games and little league
                  Fill all my time demands.

(GUESTS *exit stage right.* HOST *and* SERVANTS *enter talking, stage left. They move toward the table.*)

NARRATOR: The host could not believe it.
                  Not one had answered yes.
             The party would be such a waste
                  With not a single guest.

(HOST *and* SERVANT *have arrived at center.* SERVANTS *wait for instructions while* HOST *thinks, tapping his forehead.*)

NARRATOR: He raised a thoughtful eyebrow.
             His finger tapped his head.

HOST: I'm going to have a party.
             Invite the poor instead!

(SERVANTS *rush offstage left, followed by* HOST. *At the same time,* STREET PEOPLE *enter stage right. They take places downstage right.* SERVANT 1 *follows them in.*)

NARRATOR: His servant rushed to ask them.
             He found them on the street.

SERVANT 1:   We want you at a party
              Where there'll be lots to eat.

STREET PEOPLE: Of course, we'll come!

NARRATOR: They answered.

STREET PERSON 1: But we're not the party type.

STREET PERSON 2: No one's ever asked us.

STREET PEOPLE: Are you sure you've got this right?

(STREET PEOPLE *and* SERVANT *cross to party at center stage. If desired, more* STREET PEOPLE *enter from both sides. The* HOST *stands ready to greet them.* STREET PEOPLE *act very grateful, holding on to the* HOST'S *hand, shaking it vigorously, etc.*)

NARRATOR: They came: the poor and helpless.
                 They came to thank the host
              For throwing such a party
                 Where they were wanted most!

(NARRATOR *walks to center stage while delivering lines. Upstage, all characters are partying in a subdued manner so as not to take attention away from* NARRATOR.)

NARRATOR: Today God plans a party.
              He's already invited you.
              Will you accept and be there?

(*Everyone onstage suddenly turns toward audience.*)

ALL: Say yes, that's all you have to do!

(*All actors line up across the stage to bow.*)

Rehearsal Strategies

First Rehearsal

GETTING INTO THE ACT: 10-15 minutes
1. Set a party mood by asking early arrivers to decorate the room for a party using balloons and streamers.
2. Use the rhythm story *The Lost Coin* to engage the group in telling a story that Jesus told. Ask participants to stand. Encourage creative participation.

ACTING IT OUT: 35-40 minutes
1. Ask the group to share the best party they ever had. What would have happened if you were planning a birthday party and nobody came? Use their answers to introduce the reading of Luke 14:16-24.
2. Ask the group to make a list of characters in the story: host, servant, three guests, homeless. Decide how to divide roles evenly.
3. Use the narration as a rhythm story and lead the group, asking them to echo each line. Then, walk through the play, stanza by stanza.

TAKING THE ACT HOME: 10 minutes
1. Ask: "What is the point of the story Jesus told? What is the danger of turning down Jesus' invitation with an excuse? Where do you need to apply a lesson: by including more people in your invitations, by giving fewer excuses to Jesus?"
2. Pray together about any insights.

Second Rehearsal

GETTING INTO THE ACT: 10 minutes
1. Ask first arrivers to prepare the party decorations you will use in rehearsal.
2. Play Make a Face (see Appendix A) by asking the group to make exaggerated face expressions to respond to each of the following statements:
   a. You are invited to a party at Disneyland, all expenses paid.
   b. The day of the Disneyland party you come down with the measles!
   c. Your parents have arranged for *(name sports or TV star)* to be at your party.
   d. After you tell all your friends, your parents say "April Fools!"
      Use the exercise to talk about the importance of exaggerated facial expression, especially when acting out pantomime.

ACTING IT OUT: 40 minutes
1. Let the group list the characters in order of their appearance in the story. Characters take their beginning places. Check to see if they remember which side of the stage they enter and exit. Explain that you are going to go through the play twice. The first time, overact everything. The second time, decide how much was too much and help actors find the balance that communicates the action.

2. Talk about any costumes or props still needed and make sure assignments are clear.
3. Set performance date and time.

TAKING THE ACT HOME: 10 minutes
1. Ask questions to see if the group understands who the characters represent: Who is the host? the guests? What is the party supposed to remind us of?
2. Remind the group that the life Jesus has for us to live is a celebration worth inviting our friends to. Then, pray about it.

2

THE KINGDOM OF HEAVEN IS LIKE A . . .

(Matthew 13:31-34, 45-46; Mark 4:30-32; Luke 13:18-21)

Characters:

NARRATOR: *an adult, teen, or older child with strong stage presence*
FARMERS: 2 or more
BAKERS: 2 or more
TREASURE HUNTERS: 2 or more
PEARL DIVERS: 2 or more

Costumes:

None are necessary; however, you can add symbolic dressing. Overalls and bandannas for farmers, aprons and chef hats for BAKERS, bandanna sweat bands and small shovel for TREASURE HUNTERS, diving masks and/or snorkels for PEARL DIVERS.

Props:

Oversized Mustard Seed Package for NARRATOR

Growing Mustard Seed "trees." Simplest version can be made from strips of green paper about 36" long and 4" wide. Experiment with the best kind of paper. Construction paper is too thick. Roll the strip around a pencil. Remove the pencil and secure with tape at the bottom of the roll. With scissors, cut ⅔" down at one end of roll. Continue making cuts every ¼" until you return to your first cut. When ready to "grow" mustard plant, pull top part of fringe and gently twist out, being careful not to allow roll to cease overlapping at any point. Experiment with larger versions.

Pita bread for BAKER 1

Small loaf of bread for BAKER 2

Slice of bread for each BAKER

Ring box for NARRATOR

Play money for PEARL DIVER 1

Oversized credit card and visa for PEARL DIVER 1

Armload of favorite possessions (let actors make choices) for PEARL DIVER 2

Stage Arrangement:
Stage is empty. Actors will bring necessary props with them when they enter.

(NARRATOR *enters to stand stage center.* FARMERS *and* BAKERS *stand stage left of* NARRATOR. TREASURE HUNTERS *and* PEARL DIVERS *stand on stage right. Actors place props onstage behind them. As the parable focuses on a specific group, that group takes one step forward.*)

NARRATOR: Jesus talked a lot about the kingdom of God and nobody really understood what He meant. *(All* ACTORS *shake their heads no.)* There was the kingdom of Rome with Caesar as the king. Nobody wanted another kingdom if it was like that. (ACTORS *vigorously shake their heads and gesture with hands as if to say they want no part of Caesar's kingdom.)* But in the kingdom of God, Jesus is the King. To help people understand what belonging to His kingly rule meant, Jesus took things from ordinary life and said: "The kingdom of God is like a . . ." (NARRATOR *pauses, as if thinking.*)

ACTORS: Yes? *(Gesturing to hurry* NARRATOR *on.)*

NARRATOR: The kingdom of God is like a . . . a . . . mustard seed.

FARMERS *(looking unbelievably at each other):* A mustard seed?

FARMER 1: But they're so tiny. How could they show us anything about the kingdom of God?

NARRATOR *(takes oversized seed package and pretends to pour out seeds into the hands of each farmer):* What happens when you plant mustard seeds?

FARMERS *(shrug shoulders but take seeds, kneel, and pantomime planting)*

NARRATOR: In time the seeds grow . . .

(FARMERS *take rolled paper "trees" and make them "grow" each time* NARRATOR *says "grow.")*

NARRATOR: . . . and grow . . . and grow until they are a hundred times bigger than they were to begin with.

FARMER 1 *(beginning to understand):* You mean that the kingdom of God is something to be planted? *(Other* FARMERS *pat him on the back for getting the right answer.)*

NARRATOR: That's right. When the kingdom of God is planted in you, you let God grow in you.

(FARMERS *take a step or two back while* NARRATOR *turns to* BAKERS, *who step forward.*)

NARRATOR: But that's not all. Jesus said that the kingdom of God is like a . . . a . . . *(as if about to forget)*

ACTORS: Yes?

NARRATOR: . . . the yeast a baker uses to make bread.

BAKERS *(pantomime mixing and kneading bread, then place bread in imaginary oven behind them)*

NARRATOR: Without yeast the bread comes out . . .

(BAKER 1 *shows pita bread.* NARRATOR *examines it and shakes head.)*

NARRATOR: . . . flat!

(NARRATOR *walks to* BAKER 2, *who holds a nice-looking loaf.)*

NARRATOR: Yeast changes the dough so that bread comes out looking like this.

(BAKER 2 *smiles proudly.)*

NARRATOR: Do you understand what Jesus is trying to teach about the kingdom of God?

(BAKER 2 *has handed out slices of bread. They nod yes.)*

BAKER 1: The kingdom of God smells like bread out of the oven!

BAKER 2 *(taking a bite):* And it tastes good with lots of butter and honey on it!

NARRATOR: Well, not exactly.

(BAKERS *stop eating to listen to what* NARRATOR *says.)*

NARRATOR: The kingdom of God changes whatever it grows in, just like the yeast changes the bread dough.

BAKER 2: I still think it tastes better with butter and honey.

(BAKERS *step back and* TREASURE HUNTERS *step forward.)*

NARRATOR: Think about this: you're taking a walk in the park . . .

(TREASURE HUNTERS *mime walking, facing audience.)*

NARRATOR: . . . and suddenly you stop.

(TREASURE HUNTERS *stop immediately.)*

NARRATOR *(pointing):* Over there beside the tree . . .

(TREASURE HUNTERS *follow the point of the* NARRATOR's *hand.)*

NARRATOR: . . . something is sticking out from behind the tree.

(Puts hand to forehead in searching gesture. TREASURE HUNTERS *continue to pantomime whatever the* NARRATOR *does, as if playing follow the leader.)*

NARRATOR: You run over to the tree to see what it is.

*(*NARRATOR *and* TREASURE HUNTERS *run in place.)*

NARRATOR: You can't believe your eyes.

*(*NARRATOR *picks up imaginary box;* TREASURE HUNTERS *do the same.)*

NARRATOR: Why, this is wonderful. Not in a million years . . .

HUNTERS: *(pretend to hold a box, except they don't know what they're holding; finally ask):* What is it?

NARRATOR: Money! Thousands of dollars.

*(*TREASURE HUNTERS *look at imaginary box with different eyes and make different exclamations: Ohh! Ahh!)*

NARRATOR *(rubbing hands together in a villainous manner and getting suspiciously close to* TREASURE HUNTER 1): Now tell me. What could I do to make you give me that money?

HUNTER 1: Nothing. Nobody's getting this money. *(Pantomimes hugging treasure close to self and turns away from* NARRATOR)

*(*NARRATOR *walks to* TREASURE HUNTER 2, *who is counting things to buy.)*

HUNTER 2: Nintendo, bicycle, tape player . . .

NARRATOR: And what about you. Would you give me your money?

HUNTER 2: Absolutely not . . . Season ticket to *(add name of closest theme park).*

NARRATOR: Not even if I gave you a free trip to Disneyland?

HUNTER 2 *(thinks for a moment):* No. I'll just buy it myself.

NARRATOR: You see, that's just what Jesus said the kingdom of God is like.

HUNTERS: A trip to Disneyland?

NARRATOR: No. It's like a valuable treasure you will not give up for anything.

HUNTER 1: I'll never give this away.

HUNTER 2: Me neither.

HUNTERS: No way!

NARRATOR: That's the way. *(Giving them the go-get-'em fisted gesture.)*

*(*TREASURE HUNTERS *step back and* PEARL DIVERS *step forward.)*

NARRATOR: Jesus also compared the kingdom of God to a different kind of treasure. *(Takes a ring box out of pocket and peeks in)* Wow! Would you look at that!

DIVERS *(crowd around trying to see; all speak at once)*: What is it? Let me see. It's my turn. *(Make similar replies)*

NARRATOR: Jesus said that the kingdom of God is like a . . . *(holds waiting PEARL DIVERS in suspense)* a . . . pearl. *(Removes imaginary pearl)*

DIVERS: Ohhhhhhh!

NARRATOR: . . . a pearl so extraordinarily rare that people come from all over the world to buy it.

(NARRATOR replaces pearl and closes box. PEARL DIVERS pick up props they will use to try to buy the pearl.)

NARRATOR: But in order to buy the pearl of great price, it cost them everything they had.

DIVER 1: Here! *(Taking play money out of pockets)* I'll give you all the money I have. Not enough? Do you take Visa or MasterCard? *(Holds out both cards)*

DIVER 2: You can have my Gameboy, jam box, video collection, all my tapes, and even my dog BooBoo.

(NARRATOR accepts everything from PEARL DIVERS. DIVERS take ring box.)

NARRATOR: So the kingdom of God is a treasure that is worth giving up everything. Does that help you understand the kingdom of God?

(All stand with props and nod yes.)

FARMER 1: The kingdom of God is like a mustard seed. *(Shows seed packet)*

FARMER 2 *(holding plant)*: Because when God's kingdom is planted in us we can grow up to be like Him.

BAKER 1 *(holding slice of bread)*: The kingdom of God is like yeast.

BAKER 2 *(holding loaf)*: Because God's kingdom changes you into what God knows you can be.

HUNTER 1: The kingdom of God is like a treasure . . .

HUNTER 2: Worth finding and keeping forever.

DIVER 1 *(holding ring box)*: The kingdom of God is like an expensive pearl . . .

DIVER 2: For which you are willing to give up everything.

NARRATOR: With these stories, the people understood the kingdom of God so well . . .

(All nod yes.)

NARRATOR: . . . that they decided to join God's kingdom.

(All take a soldier's stance, salute, turn abruptly stage right, and march off singing "Onward, Christian Soldiers.")

NARRATOR: And so should you! *(Salutes. Marches after the others.)*

Rehearsal Strategies

Suggested Rehearsal Time: Three 1-hour sessions

First Rehearsal

GETTING INTO THE ACT: 10 minutes
1. Have all props gathered and on a prop table. Make sure that there is one item for each person. Explain that each item represents an occupation from the play. Play Pair Off (see Appendix A). Ask each pair to pick an item and identify the occupation. Use this activity to introduce acting parts. Affirm all responses even if they don't correspond to those from the play.
2. Ask the group to divide according to occupations. Let the groups pantomime each occupation for the whole group. Have them sit in place.

ACTING IT OUT: 40 minutes
1. Explain that Jesus used each group to teach what the kingdom of heaven is like. Then, read the story from your favorite Gospel account. Ask the group to share what they think Jesus is trying to tell us. Don't give out any answers. Let the play do that.
2. Talk through the play and then walk through it. Hand out no scripts. Simply have actors repeat lines when it is time.

TAKING THE ACT HOME: 10 minutes
1. Ask again, "What does Jesus want us to know about the kingdom of heaven?" Take time to pray about the answers. Announce the next rehearsal.

Second Rehearsal

GETTING INTO THE ACT: 15 minutes
1. As actors arrive, make the mustard seed trees using newspaper for rehearsal trees.
2. Divide into occupation groups again. Give each group a problem card to act out and make up their own ending. Assign a captain for any group over three. Allow the group five minutes to practice before sharing their scene with everyone.
Examples:

FARMERS: It started out to be a good planting day. Then, it clouded over. Soon it began to rain, then pour. What happens next?

BAKERS: You are kneading the day's bread. You put it into loaves, let it rise for an hour, then bake it. However, you forget to set the timer. What happens next?

TREASURE HUNTERS: You are using a metal detector. Suddenly it registers a find. You dig down and what do you find?

PEARL DIVERS: You dive down for a pearl. You find a clam, but it won't open. What happens next?

3. An alternative to the improvisation above is to use the rhythm story "The Sand House." Establish the echo pattern and encourage good expression by modeling it.

ACTING IT OUT: 35 minutes
1. Walk through the play again.
2. Hand out scripts. Give 5 to 10 minutes for each group to practice their lines.
3. Rehearse again.

TAKING THE ACT HOME: 10 minutes
1. Close with the same questions from the last rehearsal.
2. Pray about new understandings.
3. Announce the next rehearsal as well as performance time.

Third Rehearsal

GETTING INTO THE ACT: 10 minutes
1. Make final "trees." You might even have a poster with the title of the play outlined for children to color in with markers.
2. Play Pass It On (see Appendix A) using imaginary objects from the play: a seed, a slice of bread, a pearl. Generously affirm everyone's ideas.
3. Another way to get everyone involved in a group acting experience is by using the rhythm story, "The Rock House." Talk about its contrast to "The Sand House" and how to share that with your voice.

ACTING IT OUT: 40 minutes
1. Rehearse the play with props and full costume. Stop and talk about suggestions.
2. Rehearse again.

TAKING THE ACT HOME: 10 minutes
1. Close by asking: "What do *you* want the audience to learn from this play?" Then, pray together.
2. Identify performance time.

3

OLD MacDONALD HAD A FARM

A Pantomime Play with a Chorus

(Matthew 13:3-8; Mark 4:3-8; Luke 8:5-8)

Characters:

FARMER MACDONALD

4-8 SEEDLINGS

BIRDS (as many as there are SEEDS for the second soil group)

CHORUS (as many as you wish)

Another way to assign parts is to allow everyone a pantomime part. When not acting, they join the chorus. The only person not able to be a part of the chorus would be the FARMER.

Costumes:

Although costumes are not necessary, they are fun!

FARMER could wear overalls with a bandanna hanging out the back pocket and a straw hat on his head.

SEEDS might wear brown, pull-tie garbage bags. Cut a hole in the bottom for the head. Pull ties to gather around legs, leaving enough room to walk.

BIRDS may wear black turtlenecks and black slacks. A black semicircle cape gives the appearance of wings.

CHORUS wears blue jeans or overalls with brightly colored shirts or T-shirts. Blue and red bandannas around the neck and a few straw hats are good additions.

Props:

Poster board sign saying: Old MacDonald's Farm

Oversized seed packages labeled Sur-Gro Corn, Sur-Gro Tomatoes, Sur-Gro Green Beans

Rolled-up newspaper

Soil tester made out of 4" x 8" rectangular cardboard with "Soil Tester" on one side and "Good Soil" on the other side. Use your imagination and have fun making this.

Small poster sign saying: MacDonald's Path

Corrugated cardboard cut-out boulders and rocks designed to be self-supporting. They need to be big enough for the children playing the choked-out SEEDS to hide behind.

Corrugated cardboard cut-out thornbushes, self-supporting, also big enough for the thorn-choked SEEDS to *grow* between

Stage:

"Old MacDonald's Farm" sign is stage left near the area where SEEDS will be planted in good soil. "MacDonald's Path" sign is stage right to identify the place where seeds fell on the path. Cardboard boulders and rocks identify the rocky soil. Thornbushes identify the thorny soil. Rolled newspaper and Soil Tester can be hidden behind one of the rocks until needed. If desired, other farm tools can be scattered around. The CHORUS stands to one side to sing the verses while actors pantomime their parts.

Chorus	Actors
Old MacDonald had a farm. E—I—E—I—O!	MacDONALD *enters stage left beside the farm sign. He is carrying seed packages.*
And on his farm he had to plant. E—I—E—I—O!	MacDONALD *crosses to stage right and pantomimes throwing seeds.*
With a seed thrown here. And a seed thrown there. Here a seed! There a seed! Everywhere a little seed. Old MacDonald had a farm. E—I—E—I—O!	
Old MacDonald planted seeds. E—I—E—I—O! But some seed fell upon the path. E—I—E—I—O!	MacDONALD *continues to the area beside the path sign.* SEEDS *run and squat to indicate position.*
And a bird ate here.	BIRDS *"fly" in and nibble on* SEEDS.
And a bird ate there. Here a bird. There a bird. Everywhere a dirty bird! Ate up Old MacDonald's seed. E—I—E—I—O!	MacDONALD *uses a rolled-up newspaper to fight* BIRDS *off.* BIRDS *exit stage right dragging* SEED(s) *with them.*

Old MacDonald planted seed.
E—I—E—I—O!
But some he threw just hit the rocks.
E—I—E—I—O!
A stem grew here
But wilted there.
Here a choke!
There a choke!
Everywhere a choke, choke!
Seeds won't grow in rocky soil.
E—I—E—I—O!

Old MacDonald planted seed.
E—I—E—I—O!

Some seed fell in thorny soil.
E—I—E—I—O!
With a stickery, stick here!
And a stickery, stick there!
Here a stick!
There a stick!
Everywhere a stickery stick!
Old MacDonald planted seed
But seeds won't grown in thorns.

A frustrated MacDonald *takes seed packages again and throws toward rocks.* Seeds *run to planted position.*
Seed(s) *stretch as if waking up. Grab throat. Can't get air. Give choking cough. Finally die.*

MacDonald *shakes his head and wipes his brow.*

Again, MacDonald *plants. This time he throws toward the thorns.* Seeds *run to planted position.* Seed(s) *wake and stretch. As they do, they are stuck by thorns. They cry "ouch," "that hurts," etc. They also die melodramatically.*

Before Chorus *sings next stanza,* MacDonald *uses his Soil Tester. He puts a handful of imaginary soil in the box. Smiles and shows the audience the other side of the box that says GOOD SOIL. Confidently, he plants again.* Seed(s) *run to planted position.*

Old MacDonald planted seed.
E—I—E—I—O!
At last the seed hit good rich dirt.
E—I—E—I—O!
A plant grew here.
A plant grew there.
Here a plant!
There a plant!
Everywhere a growing plant.
Old MacDonald learned so well:
(Slowly and emphatically)
To grow, seeds need good soil!

Plants slowly wake, stretch, and continue to rise, slowly but steadily.

MacDonald *nods his head to agree.*

Rehearsal Strategies

Suggested Rehearsal Time: Two 1-hour sessions

First Rehearsal

GETTING INTO THE ACT: 10-15 minutes
1. Engage early arrivers in a Name Tag activity (see Appendix A). Ask each to make a name tag identifying something they would like to grow, real or imaginary. (Hint: chocolate, money, pizza, as well as flowers or vegetables.) Then, sit in a circle and share responses.
2. Lead a planting pantomime. Ask leading questions and ask the children to demonstrate their answers. For example: Are you working with machinery or hand tools? What is the weather like? Accept no verbal responses. Specifically affirm creative ideas.
3. Use the rhythm story "Follow! Follow!" to get everyone involved in expressing ideas using voice and face.

ACTING IT OUT: 34-40 minutes
1. Review the parable of the soils. Ask the children to name the different soils and what happens to each.
2. Divide into four groups. Within each group have the children either be seeds or part of the soil. Give the groups time to work on a brief presentation. Share the result. Keep in mind any good ideas that could be incorporated.
3. Introduce the "Old MacDonald" song and sing through it at least once. Choose a FARMER and SEEDS and BIRDS from the best pantomimes.
4. Try walking through the scenes, first without the music, then with music.

TAKING THE ACT HOME: 10 minutes
1. Close the rehearsal by discussing lessons using questions like: What is the seed Jesus talks about? What does each soil area represent in your life? What are some things that keep God's seed from growing in us?
2. Announce the next rehearsal and close with prayer.

Second Rehearsal

GETTING INTO THE ACT: 10-15 minutes
1. Have all prop signs lettered and ready to be filled in with markers or paint. Ask first-comers to work on the signs. According to the skills of your group, consider involving the children in other prop-finishing projects.
2. Review the parable by naming the soil groups.
3. Play Good Soil/Bad Soil as a warm-up game. Talk about ways to communicate the soil types with a body position. Example: Show thorny soil with clawlike fingers and mean faces. Show good soil simply by lying down with a smile on your face. Experiment together with some ideas. Then, have

everyone stand in a line facing you. Leader claps hands together once for good soil. Make a fist with one hand and pound the palm of the other hand for bad soil. Leader uses a series of three in any order. If the last is a clap, children must choose a body position for good soil. If the last is a fist in palm, children must choose a body position for bad soil. Just for fun, speed up.
4. Use "We're on the Road with Jesus" as a warm-up exercise for the Chorus. Talk about how ideas are expressed using pitch, speed, and volume.

ACTING IT OUT: 40 minutes
1. Act it out once, using Chorus and props.
2. Talk about it stanza by stanza.
3. Act it out again, trying not to stop in between stanzas.

TAKING THE ACT HOME: 5-10 minutes
1. Talk to the actors about their understanding of what makes good soil good and bad soil bad. Ask them to suggest what we should be praying for in order to be examples of good soil. Then, pray together.
2. Make plans for performance.

Optional Idea:
Have a contest to design a Soil Tester.

4

MIRACLES, SIGNS, AND WONDERS

(John 2:11; 10:25; 4:48)

Cast (7 or more):

NARRATOR: *adult, teen, or older child who is a good communicator*

SIGN HOLDERS: *Divide number to fit your group. The script calls for at least one person for each of the signs: Miracles, Signs, Wonders. Add more according to the size of your group.*

LAME MAN

BLIND MAN

DEAF MAN

SPEAKERS 1, 2, 3*: *Each shares a contemporary situation as an example of a miracle, sign, or wonder.*

These actors can also be sign holders.

Note: While this script calls for one person in each role, you may add as many children to each role as desired.

Props:

3 or more poster signs saying: God wants to save YOU! God is awesome! Get a life: Repent!

Poster signs, each with one of the following words: MIRACLES, SIGNS, WONDERS, one for each sign holder

Items to suggest each handicap: crutches, canes, sunglasses, bandages, old-fashioned-type ear horn, etc.

Costumes:

Nothing special.

Stage Arrangement:

NARRATOR stands in the center. Divide the group so that SIGN HOLDERS are on both sides of the NARRATOR. If the group is large, keep SIGN HOLDERS on the back row and other characters on the front row.

NARRATOR: When Jesus was on earth, He had one mission: to call attention to God and His good news . . . In order to accomplish this mission, Jesus used signs.

(SIGN HOLDERS *march around* NARRATOR *displaying the poster signs that say things like: God wants to save you! God is awesome! Get a life; Repent!*)

NARRATOR: No! Not signs like that. Jesus did special things called miracles.

(SIGN HOLDERS *express new understanding and put these signs away. MIRACLES* SIGN HOLDER *displays correct sign, moving stage right of* NARRATOR.)

NARRATOR: Miracles happened when God's power met someone's impossible need. *(MIRACLES sign goes down.)*

NARRATOR: They became signs to advertise God and His Good News.

(New SIGN HOLDER *displays sign that says SIGNS, standing stage left of* NARRATOR.)

NARRATOR: They were also called wonders because no one could figure them out!

(SIGNS goes down and third SIGN HOLDER *displays sign that says WONDERS, standing stage left of previous* SIGN HOLDER.)

NARRATOR: Miracles, signs, and wonders.

(SIGN HOLDERS *show all three signs.*)

NARRATOR: That's how Jesus tried to get the word out about God and His plan. As Jesus walked around on this earth, He met people with great needs. He met people who couldn't walk . . .

(LAME MAN *hobbles from stage left and stops downstage left in front of* SIGN HOLDERS.)

NARRATOR: . . . or see . . .

(BLIND MAN *enters from stage left and stops left of* LAME MAN. BLIND MAN *pretends blindness by wearing very dark sunglasses and using a cane to tap out the path.*

NARRATOR: . . . or hear.

(DEAF MAN *enters from stage right and stands downstage right of* NARRATOR. DEAF MAN *points to ears and shakes head indicating lack of hearing or uses homemade ear horn.)*

NARRATOR: And Jesus met them at the place of their greatest need. He made them walk.

LAME MAN *(drops crutches or appears to walk naturally):* I can walk! I can walk!

NARRATOR: He made them see.

BLIND MAN (*takes off sunglasses and throws cane down*): I can see! I can see!

NARRATOR: He made them hear.

DEAF MAN (*shakes head and pulls on ear with great disbelief*): I can hear! I can hear!

NARRATOR: And all the people said:

ALL: It's a miracle!

NARRATOR: And they were right. It was a miracle (SIGN HOLDER *displays MIRA-CLES sign*) to show God's power. It was a sign (SIGN HOLDER *displays SIGNS*) to point them to God! And it certainly was a wonder (SIGN HOLDER *displays WONDERS sign*) to make them worship the God of all power.

(*All signs down.*)

NARRATOR: Today, God is still working on earth through the Spirit of Jesus. He still sends miracles (*hold up MIRACLES sign*) to remind you of the power you have in God as you live your life in Christ.

SPEAKER 1: I didn't know how our family was going to make it when my dad lost his job. But we prayed for God's help. It was a miracle how Dad got some odd jobs whenever we needed money.

NARRATOR: God still uses miracles as signs (*hold up SIGNS*) to point people to God.

SPEAKER 2: When my mom got cancer I didn't know what to do except pray. We don't know what's going to happen yet, but you know what? I'm not as scared as I used to be. I really believe God cares about what happens to my family.

NARRATOR: And when God's power is at work in our lives, we all call it a wonder (*hold up sign*).

SPEAKER 3: I can't believe it. I've been praying ever since I was in kindergarten that my parents would go to church with me. Last Sunday they did. It's a miracle!

NARRATOR: Miracles, signs, and wonders. (*Hold up all signs and keep them up.*) God still wants us to know that He is the God of all power who meets all needs in ways that no one else can. So the next time God brings something special in your life, you'll know:

MIRACLES SIGN HOLDER: It's a miracle!

ALL: To show us God's power.

SIGNS HOLDER: It's a sign!

ALL: To point us to God.

WONDERS Sign Holder: It's a wonder!

All: So we can't explain it away.

Narrator: And when you know that, you'll know why the life we live in Christ is full of adventure, hope and promise . . . always!

(All bow and exit.)

Rehearsal Strategies

Suggested Rehearsal Time: Two 1-hour sessions

First Rehearsal

GETTING INTO THE ACT: 10-15 minutes

1. Ask early arrivers to make picket signs about God and the message of salvation.
2. Facilitate discussion about the messages while working together by asking: How effective are these signs in communicating the Good News? What other methods communicate? Even if you don't get any mention of miracles, use the discussion to make the point that some methods are stronger than others.

ACTING IT OUT: 35-45 minutes

1. Explain that Jesus used a powerful method to communicate the Good News: miracles. Get volunteers to read the following scriptures: John 10:25; John 2:11; John 4:48. Ask the participants to list the three words to describe Jesus' method (miracles, signs, wonders). Explain that this is the name of our play.
2. Divide into groups of two or three. Ask each group to think of a problem that people brought to Jesus. Direct them to be ready to walk across the room in such a way that shows their need without using words. Give about five minutes to practice. Then, give each group time to share their pantomime. Choose the LAME, BLIND, and DEAF actors from this exercise.
3. Choose SIGN HOLDERS and explain that they must show their sign every time you say one of the words.
4. Practice walking through the script at least once without adding the present-day miracle, sign, and wonder testimonies.

TAKING THE ACT HOME: 5-10 minutes

1. Talk about how Jesus still uses miracles, signs, and wonders today. Use the rhythm story "Jesus and His Miracles" as a summary of the message of your play. Talk about miracles from today. If possible, consider substituting some of the group's stories for the scripted testimonies. Otherwise, share the examples and identify three people who will be prepared to take the part in the next rehearsal.
2. Announce next rehearsal. Close with prayer.

Second Rehearsal

GETTING INTO THE ACT: 10-15 minutes

1. First-comers can finish signs.
2. Explain the warm-up activity Freeze Play (see Appendix A). Each person must choose an illness or handicap mentioned in the Bible. Everyone walks

around in the circle pantomiming it. When director calls "Freeze play," each actor must maintain a freeze pose. Affirm good facial expressions and body positions. Repeat a couple of times. End the Freeze Play by telling actors to pretend they have just been healed by Jesus. Have them slowly respond on the count of three. Call a last "Freeze" and ask actors to be seated in the circle. Discuss the contrast.

ACTING IT OUT: 35-40 minutes
1. Have actors get needed props and go to starting positions.
2. Rehearse with lines and props. Repeat segments until no cues are needed.
3. Go through script start to finish.

TAKING THE ACT HOME: 5-10 minutes
1. Ask the group to restate the main idea from the play. Also, be ready to share any group lessons about working together you have observed.
2. Pray for the performance.

5

A SHEEPISH STORY
or
THE PROBLEM WITH A GOATEE

(Matthew 25:31-34; John 10:3-4, 14-15)

Characters:

NARRATOR: *an expressive adult, teen, or older child*
SHEPHERD: *a Western variety, complete with bowlegs*
SHEEP: *6 or more, on all fours with plenty of baas*
2 GOATS: *sneaky in the tradition of the melodramatic villain*
OFFSTAGE VOICE(S): *to make animal sounds to scare the sheep*

Costumes:

NARRATOR wears regular street clothes.
SHEPHERD wears jeans, western shirt, cowboy belt, and hat.
SHEEP, consider using home-made or purchased sheep masks to identify sheep.
GOATS can have horns attached by headbands and "goatee" beards made from a wig or yarn. Goats also need two baseball caps, which they use to try to hide their horns.

Props:

Two bandannas for masks
Stool for NARRATOR
Extralarge folder for NARRATOR to place script in with title of play clearly printed on outside

(NARRATOR *enters and sits on the stool down right stage.*)

NARRATOR: Jesus told many stories while He was on earth. All of them explained special lessons. See if you can figure out the lesson in this story. *(Opens folder and begins reading.)* Once upon a time there was a man who had a herd of sheep.

(SHEPHERD *enters stage left while* SHEEP *enter stage right. They stay on opposite sides of the stage.*)

SHEPHERD: I am the shepherd.

SHEEP: We are the sheep.

NARRATOR: Every day at sundown, the shepherd would call his sheep.

SHEPHERD: Here sheepy, sheepy, sheep. Come here to Daddy-poo!

NARRATOR: And immediately the sheep would come running.

(SHEEP *run over to* SHEPHERD *and almost knock him down.*)

SHEPHERD: Whoa! Hold on! Calm down!

NARRATOR: The shepherd would open the gate and let all the sheep go in. Here they would be safe from the wolves . . .

OFFSTAGE: O-UUUUUUUUUUUUU!

(Each time the offstage sounds are heard, sheep hug each other and shiver while SHEPHERD pets each one and calms them.)

NARRATOR: . . . and lions . . .

OFFSTAGE: GRRRRROOOOOAAARR!

NARRATOR: . . . and all the other dangers of the night.

OFFSTAGE: O-UUUUUUUUUU! GRRRROOOOOAAARRR! EEEOOOOW! WHOOOOOOOO!

NARRATOR: One by one the shepherd would let the sheep into the pen, calling each by name . . .

(SHEPHERD *opens imaginary gate. One by one* SHEEP *go in as a name is called.* SHEEP *can circle back behind* SHEPHERD *and enter again to give the appearance of many more sheep.*)

SHEPHERD: Adam, Betty, Carla, Deedra, Ethel, Frank, Gus, Hattie, Ila, Jacob . . .

NARRATOR: . . . until each one was safely in.

SHEPHERD *(with finality):* Zane.

NARRATOR: When the sheep were safe, the shepherd could go to bed and sleep as well.

(SHEPHERD *lays down in front of sheep and snores.*)

NARRATOR: Sometimes, some neighborhood goats would hide near the gate and be ready to slip in with the sheep when the shepherd opened the gate the next morning.

(GOATS *enter and hide by crouching.* SHEPHERD *wakes, stretches, and stands to open gate.* GOATS *slip in with* SHEEP *while* SHEPHERD *is looking the other way.* GOATS *and* SHEEP *cross stage right.*)

NARRATOR: But at the end of the day, when the sheep come back to the fold, the shepherd is there to make sure only his sheep get into the fold.

(SHEEP *and* GOATS *cross back to where* SHEPHERD *waits at the gate. This time the* GOATS *are fifth and sixth in line.*)

SHEPHERD: Adam, Betty, Carla, Deedra . . . who are you?

GOAT 1: Would you believe Deedra's cousin?

SHEPHERD: No, I wouldn't. You're no sheep of mine. In fact, you aren't anybody's sheep. You are goats.

GOAT 2 (*stroking beard*): Look, so we have a little extra facial hair. What's the big deal? We chew our grass the same way!

GOAT 1: Yeah!

SHEPHERD: But that's not the point!

NARRATOR: The shepherd tried to explain.

(SHEPHERD *pantomimes talking to* GOATS. SHEEP *affirm everything the* NARRATOR *says by shaking or nodding their heads in agreement.*)

NARRATOR: He told the goats that his sheep know his voice. His sheep follow him wherever he goes. "There is no place in the sheep pen for goats," the shepherd said. And with that, he pushed the goats away so that his sheep could enter the pen. (SHEPHERD *pushes* GOATS *out of pen.*) But the goats weren't to be turned out so easily.

GOATS: Nobody tells us where to get off!

NARRATOR: They decided to try to camouflage their telltale goat characteristics.

GOATS (*They tie bandannas to hide their chin beards and try to push their horns inside baseball caps. While doing so, they cover their movements with ad-lib statements like: What do you think? Will this work. Why not? etc.*)

NARRATOR: Then, they joined the sheep when the shepherd let them out to graze. (GOATS *cross to* SHEEP. SHEPHERD *directs* SHEEP *out and* GOATS *slip in, unnoticed.* SHEEP *and* GOATS *cross stage left.*) The sheep didn't know the difference. At the end of the day, when the shepherd came to call the sheep . . .

SHEPHERD: Here sheepy, sheepy, sheep. Come to Daddy-poo.

NARRATOR: . . . the sheep came running.

(SHEEP *come running, almost knocking* SHEPHERD *down.* GOATS *nearly miss the cue.*)

SHEPHERD: All right, already. Now, into the pen with you.

NARRATOR: And he called them by name.

(SHEEP *line up in same order as before with* GOATS *in places five and six.*)

SHEPHERD: Adam, Betty, Carla, Deedra, Ethel . . . wait a minute. You're not Ethel.

GOAT 1: Sure I am. (*Clears voice and then changes to a high-pitched female voice*) I mean, sure I am.

SHEPHERD (*suspiciously*): What's with the cap, Ethel?

GOAT 1: It's to protect my lambskin face from the sun.

SHEPHERD (*to* GOAT 2): And the bandanna?

GOAT 2 (*also in a high-pitched voice*): A toothache. That's right. It's a toothache. Been bothering me all day.

SHEPHERD: Sure. You can't fool me. (*Takes off the caps and bandannas to reveal horns and beards*) You're nothing but old goats. Now get out of here!

NARRATOR: The goats pleaded.

(GOATS *kneel in begging posture.*)

NARRATOR: They tried to convince the shepherd that they were distant cousins. After all, they ate like sheep, walked like sheep, slept like sheep. Why, they were practically sheep. But the shepherd was unbending.

SHEPHERD: You're out of here now, or I'll have barbecued goat for dinner tonight.

(GOATS *cross far left.*)

NARRATOR: The shepherd turned back to his sheep and continued naming them:

SHEPHERD: Ethel. Frank. Gus. Hattie . . .

NARRATOR: And when he was through . . .

SHEPHERD: Zane.

NARRATOR: He closed the gate and said to his sheep:

SHEPHERD: I am your shepherd.

SHEEP: And we are the sheep of your pasture.

SHEPHERD: Get some sleep.

NARRATOR: And so they did. Now you may wonder what a story about sheep and goats has to do with Jesus. Well, it's like this. If you want a safe place for the rest of your eternal life, you need to be like the sheep following the Shepherd Jesus.

(SHEEP *raise their heads and nod yes and go back to sleep.*)

NARRATOR: . . . not like the goats who pretended to be sheep.

GOATS: Yeah! Boy did we blow it!

NARRATOR: The shepherd always knows the difference!

(SHEPHERD *wakes up and nods his head and then goes back to sleep. Everyone snores loudly.*)

NARRATOR: The end.

(*Bows. Motions for* SHEPHERD *and* SHEEP *to take a bow while* GOATS *tiptoe across to join them. They are discovered by the* SHEPHERD, *who chases them offstage, followed by the* SHEEP *and* NARRATOR.)

Rehearsal Strategies

Suggested Rehearsal Time: Two 1-hour sessions

First Rehearsal

GETTING INTO THE ACT: 10 minutes

1. As participants arrive, give each an index card with a line from a children's song or story about sheep or goats. Allow three cards of a kind. Examples: Sing: "Mary Had a Little Lamb." Call out the phrase "Three Billy Goats Gruff." Sing "Baa Baa Black Sheep, Have You Any Wool?" Call out, "Little Bo Peep Has Lost Her Sheep." On cue, everyone is to say or sing what is on the card at the same time, in order to find other members of their group.
2. When groups have been identified, they are to put together a one-minute pantomime that identifies the key characters in each song or story without having to retell the whole story. Give no more than five minutes to rehearse. Then, share the pantomimes with the whole group.

ACTING IT OUT

1. Explain that the Bible uses sheep and goats as symbols to teach a lesson about being a Christian. Read the scripture focus: Matthew 25:31-34 and John 10:3-4, 14-15. Help the children to identify the way the sheep respond to the shepherd. Make a list on a chalkboard to refer back to when working on characterization.
2. From the earlier pantomimes, identify those who will play the sheep, goats, and the shepherd.
3. Identify the stage areas. Walk through the script. Ask actors to repeat lines after you to familiarize them with speaking parts.

TAKING THE ACT HOME

1. Ask the group to identify who the sheep, shepherd, and goats represent in the story. How can we show that we are sheep instead of goats? Use responses to pray a closing prayer.
2. Announce the next rehearsal.

Second Rehearsal

GETTING INTO THE ACT

1. If you plan to use masks or costumes, use the beginning moments to hand them out and let the actors experiment with them.
2. Play an adapted version of Animal Walk (see Appendix A), using only sheep and goats to work on specific characterization goals. Talk about the way to distinguish between the ways goats and sheep walk and move their heads, etc.
3. Another opening activity is to play one of the memorization review games listed in Appendix A.

ACTING IT OUT
1. Move to stage positions. Walk through the script, scene by scene. Repeat the scene until action and lines happen without cues from you.
2. Sit down in a circle and ask each actor to think of something that someone else did well. When all participants have received a specific affirmation, try going through the play from start to finish.
3. Announce the performance time and details.

TAKING THE ACT HOME
1. Review who each of the characters represent from the play. Ask, "Why can't the goats hang out with the sheep in Jesus' story? Why can the shepherd spot the goats when the sheep can't?" Pray about application lessons and the opportunity to share them in a performance.

6

YOU CAN CHOOSE

(Matthew 5:1-11)

This sketch involves carefully sequenced action, planned to emphasize the rhythmic beat of the poem. In order to get the main idea of the sketch, read the poem before studying the action. Emphasize the underlined word to achieve predictable rhythm. Then, read the Rehearsal Strategies through, being sure to study Appendix B. It will help you understand how the action synchronizes with the poem. Stanzas are numbered to help with rehearsal instructions. Letters A-F identify stage placement formations. You will find illustrations of these formations in Appendix B.

Characters:

NARRATOR OR CHORUS: *Either a single reader, preferably an adult, or use a group of readers that an adult leads.*

HAPPY FACES: *Half of the actors in the Action group who usually show the happy face of their hand-held, reversible happy-sad face mask.*

SAD FACES: *The other half of the actors in the Action group who usually show the sad face of their hand-held, happy-sad face mask.*

Props:

Happy-Sad Face masks for each member of the Action group

To make: Draw a happy face on a Styrofoam plate using a permanent black marker. To make it reversible, flip it over and draw another smile. (See Examples A and B.) Use a cool glue gun to connect a craft or paint stick to the plate so that half can be held as Happy Faces and the other half as Sad Faces.

A Happy Face

B Sad Face

Jesus Picture
>Glue a picture of Jesus' face on the back of one of the Happy Face masks. Give to the actor who stands nearest the center.

One Way Signs, also hand-held
>You will need one for each of the Happy Face sign holders.

First Aid Kits for use in stanza 13 with easy-to-apply Band-Aids or bandages.

Large red hearts on the back of all masks except for Jesus.

Stage Arrangement:

There are six basic formations for this play, lettered A-F. Formations place actors in one or two rows. In a two-row placement, only front row masks should be visible to the audience. See Appendix B for illustrations. The lettered formations appear on the Action side as a sample row of five Happy Faces and five Sad Faces, as they appear in Appendix B. You will find complete instructions about how to introduce and sequence teaching these formations in Rehearsal Strategies. The CHORUS or NARRATOR stands to one side of the face mask holders. They read the lines emphasizing a pronounced two-beat rhythm. The underlined syllables indicate this rhythm. Clapping may help, but be sure it does not get in the way of good pronunciation. Also, make sure the CHORUS doesn't go so fast that the Action group has trouble keeping up.

Chorus	Action
1:	*Formation changes on each line.*
You can <u>choose</u> to be <u>happy</u>.	(A) ☹☹☹☹☹ ☺☺☺☺☺
You can <u>choose</u> to be <u>sad</u>. <u>help</u>er.	(B) ☺☺☺☺☺ ☹☹☹☹☹
You can <u>choose</u> to be a	(A) ☹☹☹☹☹ ☺☺☺☺☺
You can <u>choose</u> to be <u>bad</u>.	(B) ☺☺☺☺☺ ☹☹☹☹☹
2:	
It's what <u>Je</u>sus tried to <u>teach</u> us	(C) ☺☺☺☺☺✝☺☺☺☺
In the <u>ser</u>mon on the <u>mount</u>,	*Center person holds picture of Jesus.*

And we'd like to share it
with you.

You can help us keep a count.

*The rest point to picture
and then to audience.*

3:

You can be a kingdom-liver

(E) ☺○☺○☺○☺○☺○

In a happy, humble way.

Sad Faces turn with backs to audience.

Choosing God as first adviser,

Happy Faces point heavenward.

Letting Him have His first say.

4:

You can also shun God's kingdom.

(B) ☺☺☺☺☺

Make yourself the central dude.

☹☹☹☹☹

Speak your mind when it's
 convenient,

*Sad Faces strut and point to
selves.*

Even when your thoughts are rude.

5:

And when your heart is heavy,

(D) ☺☹☺☹☺☹☺☹☺☹

And when your world is sad,
God can bring His special comfort.

*Happy Faces console Sad Faces until
all are changed to happy on last line.*

Choosing Him can make you glad.

(F) ☺☺☺☺☺☺☺☺☺☺

6:

Turn God's happy way of living

(E) ☺○☺○☺○☺○☺○

Upside-down and you will see,

(D) ☺☹☺☹☺☹☺☹☺☹

You can choose a pouty spirit

On second line, Sad Faces turn around.

If that's who you want to be.

7:

Repeat from stanza 1:

You can choose to be happy.

(A) ☹☹☹☹☹
    ☺☺☺☺☺

You can choose to be sad.

(B) ☺☺☺☺☺
    ☹☹☹☹☹

You can <u>choose</u> to be a <u>help</u>er.   *Repeat A.*

You can <u>choose</u> to be <u>bad</u>.   *Repeat B.*

8:

It's what <u>J</u>esus tried to <u>teach</u> us   (C) ☺☺☺☺☺✝☺☺☺☺

In His <u>ser</u>mon long ag<u>o</u>.   *Center person shows picture of Jesus
while the rest point to it. On last line,
everyone points to audience.*

And we're <u>here</u> to share it <u>with</u> you.

To be <u>sure</u> it's what you <u>know</u>.

9:

Others <u>first</u> is also <u>living</u>   (D, *with space between couples*)

Just how <u>J</u>esus called us <u>to</u>.   ☺☹☺☹☺☹☺☹☺☹

It's a <u>choice</u>. He calls it <u>meek</u>ness   (B) ☺☺☺☺☺

But the <u>ones</u> who choose are <u>few</u>.   ☹☹☹☹☹
*Happy Faces signal to Sad Faces to go
first while Sad Faces point to themselves,
as if questioning and step forward.*

10:

Yes, the <u>choice</u> for right
way <u>living</u>   (A) ☹☹☹☹☹
  ☺☺☺☺☺

Is a <u>deep</u> desire to <u>live</u>   *Happy Faces rub stomachs as if hungry.*

Wanting <u>God</u> so much you <u>feel</u> it

Like the <u>signs</u> a hunger <u>gives</u>.

11:

You can <u>choose</u> the wrong way
<u>eas</u>'ly.   (D) ☺☹☺☹☺☹☺☹☺☹

No one <u>for</u>ces you, you <u>know</u>.   *Happy Faces show road signs. Sad Faces
move opposite to signs.*
Go the <u>wrong</u> way on a <u>one</u> way
And you <u>crash</u>. You know it's <u>so</u>.

12:

You can <u>choose</u> to be <u>happy</u>.

Change formation for each line.

(A) ☹☹☹☹☹
   ☺☺☺☺☺

You can <u>choose</u> to be <u>sad</u>.

(B) ☺☺☺☺☺
   ☹☹☹☹☹

You can <u>choose</u> to be a <u>help</u>er.

Repeat A.

You can <u>choose</u> to be <u>bad</u>.

Repeat B.

13:

It's what <u>Jesus</u> tried to <u>teach</u> us

(C) ☺☺☺☺☺✝☺☺☺☺

In His <u>sermon</u> long ag<u>o</u>.

Center person holds picture of Jesus and rest point first to Jesus and then to audience.

And we're <u>here</u> to share it <u>with</u> you

To be <u>sure</u> it's what you <u>know</u>.

14:

You can <u>be</u> a mercy-gi<u>ver</u>,

(D) *with space between couples.*

Sharing <u>love</u>, forgiveness <u>too</u>.

☺☹☺☹☺☹☺☹☺☹

In the <u>action</u> of your <u>giving</u>,

Happy Faces give care to Sad Faces from first aid kits: Band-Aids, etc. Use quick, easy-to-complete ideas.

You re<u>ceive</u> some mercy <u>too</u>.

15:

You can <u>fight</u> for twisted <u>fairness</u>,

(B) ☺☺☺☺☺
   ☹☹☹☹☹

Making <u>sure</u> it's fair for <u>you</u>.

Grabbing <u>rights</u> that hurt an<u>other</u>,

Sad Faces argue to the point of push and shove. They end in a freeze.

After <u>all</u>, who cares, do <u>you</u>?

16:

You can <u>choose</u> a kind of <u>clean</u>ness,

Inside <u>out</u>, a heart that's <u>pure</u>.

Then, you <u>see</u> the God you're <u>serv</u>ing

With this <u>20</u>-20 <u>cure</u>.

(C) ☺☺☺☺☺✝☺☺☺☺

All masks turn to show hearts and Jesus picture.

17:

Change formation with each line.

You can <u>choose</u> to be <u>happy</u>.

(A) ☹☹☹☹☹
   ☺☺☺☺☺

You can <u>choose</u> to <u>sad</u>.

(B) ☺☺☺☺☺
   ☹☹☹☹☹

You can <u>choose</u> to be a <u>help</u>er.

Repeat A.

You can <u>choose</u> to be <u>bad</u>.

Repeat B.

18:

You can <u>choose</u> this happy <u>living</u>.

(A) ☹☹☹☹☹
   ☺☺☺☺☺

You can <u>choose</u>; don't pass it <u>by</u>.

(D) ☺☹☺☹☺☹☺☹☺☹

You can <u>choose</u>. No one will <u>force</u> you.

Sad Faces step forward and appear to be thinking about the choice.

You can <u>choose</u>, so why not <u>try</u>.

(F) ☺☺☺☺☺☺☺☺☺☺
On last line, Sad Faces change to happy faces. All bow.

Rehearsal Strategies

Suggested Rehearsal Time: Three 1-hour sessions

Rehearsal Materials:

Make rehearsal posters picturing each lettered formation from Appendix B. On a separate poster, make a master chart showing two lines of circles equal to the possible number of participants. Draw Happy Faces on front row and Sad Faces on back row. Leave room under the circle to write the name of the actor who will fill each place. See example in Appendix B.

First Rehearsal

GETTING INTO THE ACT: 5-10 minutes

1. Have each participant make the reversible happy-sad face on a paper plate. These will be practice props. Encourage positive sharing about good things from the day or week.
2. Divide the group into couples, even if it means you pair with one. Then play Mirror. Let the person whose birthday is closest to the day be the leader. Couples face each other, arms up with palms out, without touching each other. The leader emphasizes movement above the waist, including facial expression. The partner acts as his mirror. After everyone tries it, consider asking one or two volunteer teams to demonstrate for the whole group.

ACTING IT OUT: 40-45 minutes

1. Present the subject of the play by talking about following Jesus as a kind of Mirror activity. Explain that Jesus gives us clues about how to mirror His actions in the Sermon on the Mount, especially the Beatitudes.
2. Pass out scripts, asking participants to share. Then, read through the first two stanzas, demonstrating the importance of vocal expression and rhythm. Begin again, asking the whole group to read the script, stanza by stanza, using good expression and rhythm. If you are looking for a possible narrator or group of unison voices, this is a good time to try out some possibilities. Separate this group out before the next step.
3. Begin working on the Action by asking the rest to get into Mirror pairs again with their paper plate reversible faces. Adjust groups as necessary, identifying new leaders if needed. If the duets have changed dramatically, go through a quick Mirror exercise.
4. Introduce position A as Home Base. This makes it easy to get actors into starting position for announcements or instructions. Ask Mirror leaders to stand on the front row and show Happy Faces. Ask Mirror followers to stand behind with Sad Faces. Then, fill out the master lineup poster to reflect this order.
5. Introduce position C: working on specific instructions for moving from one

position to another. (Example: Happy Faces always step to back row on the left of Sad Faces, and Sad Faces step forward on the right. Use this same rule when making a straight line. Work on learning the first three most used positions. (If using a unison CHORUS, get helpers to hold the sign cards prepared for each numbered formation.)

6. Practice movement and motions with the first two stanzas, using position cue cards.
7. Introduce each position. Practice position order for stanzas 1-8 without narration, almost like a game. Show cue cards and observe how actors get into place. Then, practice with the reading of the stanzas. If time allows, go through the sequence again. Don't work for perfection, just familiarity with the order.

TAKING THE ACT HOME: 10 minutes
1. Ask actors to get a Bible and turn to the Beatitudes in Matthew 5:1-11. Ask them to identify the specific Beatitudes paraphrased in the stanzas. Talk about real-life examples of mirroring these be-attitudes.
2. Announce the next rehearsal. Close with prayer.

Second Rehearsal

GETTING INTO THE ACT: 10 minutes
1. Encourage first-comers to review stage positions. When everyone is together, use a variation of the game, Director Says, by calling out position numbers and giving actors a chance to get into place. Throw in wrong numbers. Speed up the number-calling for fun. Make a note of any problems you detect. (If using a CHORUS, let them take turns playing director.)

ACTING IT OUT: 40-45 minutes
1. Consider enlisting a helper who could work with NARRATOR or CHORUS on rhythm, expression, and enunciation. Use any of the rhythm stories to help practice vocal expression. Consider approaching the CHORUS script as a rhythm story and allow the group to echo the leader.
2. Review the stage positions and actions with the first eight stanzas.
3. Practice new material again.
4. Start over. This time add other props and specially made hand masks. Reunite with NARRATOR or CHORUS. Work for easy transition between stanzas, specially the stanzas requiring props. Practice problem stanzas one more time before closing rehearsal.

TAKING THE ACT HOME: 10-15 minutes
1. Divide into groups of two to three. Assign one or two Beatitudes from Matthew 5:1-11, asking the group to match their verse(s) with one of the stanzas from the play. Share with whole group as time allows.
2. Ask leading questions to push toward application. Example: Which attitude is the hardest to mirror? Which attitude have you seen an example of this week? Which attitude do you need to work on the most? Which attitudes have you seen during rehearsal?
3. Close with a group Mirror exercise that you lead. Then, remind them that

we are to mirror Jesus' words from the Sermon on the Mount, not just in the play, but in real life.
4. Ask for some volunteer sentence prayers or lead in prayer yourself.

Third Rehearsal

GETTING INTO THE ACT: 5-10 minutes
1. If possible, this rehearsal should take place on the performance stage. Involve early arrivers to place props.
2. Use the game from last week to review all positions. Variation: Have NARRATOR or CHORUS choose a stanza to read and see if actors remember correct position.

ACTING IT OUT: 40-45 minutes
1. Rehearse stanzas where action or transition needs strengthening. Then, start at the beginning and try to go all the way through without stopping.
2. Be sure to practice how to walk onstage and how to leave.
3. Make sure performance time is clear to all. Agree on where to meet and how to practice at least once before performance.

TAKING THE ACT HOME: 5-10 minutes
1. Ask what the audience should remember about "You Can Choose." Talk to the group about *being* the Bible for their audience. What will help the audience really hear the message?
2. Close by praying sentence prayers about being a part of making God's Word come to life with their performance.

Group-Participation Drama

USING GROUP-PARTICIPATION DRAMA

For Practice or Performance

Group-participation stories are especially helpful when working with children. It's a way to get everyone in on the act. They allow children to experiment freely with expression without realizing it. Any form of a story that allows simultaneous group enactment falls into this category. Two special methods appear in this collection: rhythm stories and audience-participation stories.

Rhythm Stories

Rhythm stories are stories in rhyme that require participants to echo each line. They have very predictable, even singsong rhythm. It helps to emphasize the rhythm through clapping. The leader speaks the first line with appropriate inflection. Participants simply repeat it using similar inflection. Stories allow participants to experiment with variety in speed, volume, even pitch. The rhythm story could be thought of as a forerunner to rap. The difference between rhythm stories and rap is that rap does not use an echo response and rap rhythm is generally more complicated, emphasizing syncopation.

Use rhythm stories in rehearsal warm-up to give every participant good experiences in expressing ideas with vocal variety. You can also use rhythm stories for an audience. You will find ideas for performance at the end of each selection.

Audience-Participation Stories

These are narratives that assign certain identifying phrases to different characters. Divide your group by the characters in the story. Each time the narrator reads the character's name, the group responds with its phrase or sound. It's a fun exercise with which to talk about characterization by what they say and how they say it. When used for an audience, the participants lead the audience in their responses. Especially in this setting, simple props or costumes make the presentation more interesting.

1

UNDER CONSTRUCTION

An Audience-Participation Story

(Matthew 7:24-27; Luke 6:47-49)

Assign the following sounds to different groups in your audience or class. Use the adjoining cue words as the signal for these sounds. Because there are so many sound groups, this is a good piece to have your actors share with a larger audience.

Cue Word	Sound
"Built"	Hammer and saw sounds
"First Builder"	*A Ha!*
"Dig"	*Uhhh!*
"Storm"	Wind and rain sounds together
"Wind"	*Whhheww!*
"Rain"	*Shhhhhhhh!*
"Second Builder"	*Uh-oh!*
"Rock"	Slap with hands
"Sand"	*Splat!* (spoken)

The Story

Jesus told many stories while He was on earth. One of His stories was about two men who **BUILT** a house for their families. The **FIRST BUILDER** took a shovel and began to **DIG**. He continued to **DIG** and **DIG** until he found **ROCK**. The **FIRST BUILDER BUILT** his house to stand up during any kind of **STORM**.

The **SECOND BUILDER** was not like the **FIRST BUILDER**. The **SECOND BUILDER** didn't **DIG** and **DIG** to find **ROCK**. The **SECOND BUILDER** found a place with some **SAND**. "That's good enough for me," said the **SECOND BUILDER**. So that's where he **BUILT** his house.

When his house was **BUILT,** a **STORM** came. The **STORM** had high

WINDS and heavy **RAINS.** It was such a bad **STORM** that many called it a flood. The **FIRST BUILDER** was safe inside the house he **BUILT** on **ROCK.** But the **SECOND BUILDER** was afraid to be in the house he **BUILT** on **SAND.** The **SECOND BUILDER** ran out just as a the **WIND** blew his house down.

Jesus doesn't want us to be like the **SECOND BUILDER** who **BUILT** his house on **SAND.** He wants us to be like the **FIRST BUILDER** who **BUILT** his house on **ROCK.**

2

THE UNFORGIVING SERVANT

An Audience-Participation Story

(Matthew 18:23-34)

Divide the audience into the following groups and assign them the responses corresponding to their character. Each time the storyteller mentions the name of the character, those assigned to that character sound make the appropriate response. It is helpful to choose a leader for each group. Simple props for each leader add to the fun.

Character	Sound
Storyteller	One person who reads the story with appropriate pauses for audience response.
King	*Ta-da-ta-da!* (as if making a trumpet announcement)
Money	Gimmee, gimmee, gimmee!
Servant	Yes Sir!
Time	Tick-tock; Tick-tock!
Unforgiving Servant	Booooo!

Props:

Use a fast food crown for the **KING**
Play money for **MONEY** leader
An alarm clock for the **TIME** leader
Apron and/or broom for **SERVANT**
A waiter's towel over the arm for the **UNFORGIVING SERVANT**

The Story

Once there was a **KING.** He was in his **MONEY**-counting room when he realized that one of his **SERVANTS** owed him some **MONEY.** This **SERVANT** owed him a lot of **MONEY**: $10,000 to be exact. So the **KING** called for his **SERVANT** to be brought to him.

When the **SERVANT** came before the **KING,** the **KING** said: "You owe me some **MONEY.** When can you pay me the **MONEY?**" The **SERVANT** fell to his knees, "But I can't pay you the **MONEY,**" the **SERVANT** cried. So the **KING** ordered that the **SERVANT** and his family be put in prison.

"Oh please, please don't do that!" the **SERVANT** sobbed. "I'll pay you the **MONEY.** Just give me some more **TIME.**"

The **KING** saw his brokenhearted **SERVANT** and changed his mind. The **KING** said to his **SERVANT:** "I can't put you in prison. I can't put your family in prison, just because of **MONEY.** Never mind about more **TIME.** Just forget about the **MONEY** you owe me.

His **SERVANT** couldn't believe his ears. "Thank you! Oh, thank you, my **KING!**" And the **SERVANT** went away happy.

As this **SERVANT** was leaving, he met up with another **SERVANT** who owed him some **MONEY.** How much **MONEY?** Only $100. But the first **SERVANT** grabbed the second **SERVANT** and began to choke him. "You owe me some **MONEY** and I want you to pay me today!"

The second **SERVANT** fell to his knees and begged: "Please give me some **TIME** and I will pay you back."

But the first **SERVANT** was an **UNFORGIVING SERVANT,** and he had the man put in prison until the **MONEY** was paid.

When the other **SERVANTS** saw what happened they reported it to the **KING.** So the **KING** called the **UNFORGIVING SERVANT** to appear before him and the **KING** said: "You wicked **UNFORGIVING SERVANT.** I canceled the **MONEY** you owed me because you begged me to. But when you saw another **SERVANT** who owed you **MONEY,** you didn't show the same kindness I showed you. Because you are an **UNFORGIVING SERVANT,** you will go to prison where you will stay for as much **TIME** as it takes to pay me all the **MONEY** you owe me. Then, maybe you will learn what it means to be a **SERVANT** of the **KING.**

3

WE'RE ON THE ROAD WITH JESUS

Clap on boldface words or syllables. Each line takes two claps. Keep the rhythm steady and consistent.

Emphasize words and phrases that carry visual images or indicate action with your voice and face.

The "On the Road . . ." series also allows you to march to the beat, if it is consistent with the story.

Establish the rhythm so that you emphasize the boldface syllable with the right foot each time.

Consider alternating between clapping and marching. However, if marching becomes a distraction, then stick with clapping.

Remember, rhythm stories are echo stories. The leader starts the clapping rhythm, then says the first line and waits for the group to echo it.

We're **on** the road with **Je**sus.
  We're **walk**ing sandal **feet**.
The **sun** is hot and **blist**ery.
  Some **wat**er would be **sweet**.

We're **on** the road with **Je**sus.
  He's **sent** us every**one**.
He **wants** us for his **wit**ness.
  We're **go**ing to follow the **Son**.

We're **on** the road with **Je**sus.
  We'll **fol**low every**day**.
Wher**ev**er he might **lead** us.
  We're **with** Him all the **way**.

We're **on** the road with **Je**sus.
  And **as** we leave this **place**.
It's **Je**sus that we **fol**low
  With **smiles** upon our **face**.

Performance Idea:

Dress in Bible costumes like disciples. Face audience and step in place to rhythm. A leader-narrator reads the first line and actors echo it. Use facial expression and body posture to reflect the word images. Example: For "The sun is hot and blistery," actors visibly sag, showing effects of heat. After last line, actors turn toward exiting direction.

Narrator repeats the last two lines while actors repeat on the way offstage, smiling of course.

4

WHEN JESUS STILLS THE STORM

Note previous clapping instructions.

We're **on** the road with **Jesus**.
   Do you **wan**na come a**long**?
You've **got** to follow **close**ly.
   You've **got** to sing His **song.**

We're **on** the road with **Jesus**.
   We're **com**ing to a **lake**.
A **boat** is waiting **for** us
   The **other** side to **take**.

We're **in** the boat with **Jesus**
   And **row**ing side by **side.**
The **clouds** are getting **angry**.
   "Row **har**der," Peter **cried**.

(Increase speed.)
We're **row**ing fast and **fur**ious.
   We're **row**ing for our **lives.**
It **does**n't look so **hope**ful
   That **we** will all sur**vive!**

We're **in** a storm with **Jesus**.
   The **boat** begins to **fill**.
And **just** when things are **hope**less:
   Our **Lord** cries, "Peace! Be **still!**" *(slower and softer)*
(Repeat the last two lines for emphasis.)

We're **in** the calm with **Jesus**:
   (Gentler) The **Lord** of wind and **waves.**
We **won't** fear any **prob**lem
   For **He's** the One who **saves**.
(Repeat the last two lines for effect, if desired.)

Performance Idea:

Instead of presenting this as a rhythm story, consider making it a pantomime with a narrator. Select biblical costumes, varied colors for disciples and white for the Jesus character.

Jesus is at the front of the line, all facing right stage and walking in place. On first two stanzas, disciples act as if inviting the audience. A cutout cardboard rowboat is upstage behind them.

At stanza 3, Jesus leads disciples to the rowboat.

At stanza 4, all pick it up and four disciples pick up cardboard oars to row.

During "storm" they row harder while boat rocks severely. Select one disciple to be Peter. Pantomime panic and bailing as boat fills with water.

On cue, Jesus holds out hands to command calm.

Disciples show amazement and relief.

On last stanza, disciples row, exiting left, still in boat.

5

JESUS AND HIS MIRACLES

See previous instructions.

We're **on** the road with **Je**sus.
    We **fol**low closely **by**.
We **see** His acts of **mer**cy.
    We **feel** His loving **sigh**.

We're **on** the road with **Je**sus.
    We **see** the crowds that **press**.
They **come** with every **prob**lem
    For **Je**sus to ad**dress**.

They **come** as blind and **crip**pled;
    They **come** as deaf and **dumb**;
They've **suf**fered great re**jec**tion;
    They **feel** like dirty **scum**.

They **want** a touch from **Je**sus;
    They **want** to find re**lief**;
And **ev**ery time the **Mas**ter
    Gives **heal**ing with be**lief**.

We're **on** the road with **Je**sus.
    Not **long** ago, but **now**
He in**vites** us with our **prob**lems
    To **come** to Him and **bow**.

We're **on** the road with **Je**sus.
    There's **mir**acles every **day**.
If **we** just let Him **guide** us
    And **al**ways live His **way**.
    (Repeat last two lines for emphasis, if desired.)

Performance Idea:

Use a narration chorus, 5 to 10 individuals with expressive voices who will read the poem while others pantomime. They may add the clapping rhythm if desired.

6

JESUS, THE STORM-STILLER

(Matthew 8:23-27; Mark 4:37-41; Luke 8:22-25)

See previous instructions.

It was **get**ting close to **sun**down
  By the **Lake** of Gali**lee**,
And **Je**sus was there **speak**ing
  Telling **peo**ple how to **be**.

He had **told** them simple **stor**ies
  About **lamps** and growing **seeds**.
And they **list**ened quite in**tent**ly
  'Til His **mes**sage met their **need**.

As they **left** to make their **jour**ney
  To their **homes** some miles a**way**.
Jesus **spoke** to His dis**ci**ples
  As the **sun** gave weakened **rays**.

"Let us **leave** this shore," He **told** them.
  "Travel **to** the other **side**."
So they **took** a boat and **board**ed
  For the **gen**tle lake-length **ride**.

Jesus, **tired** and very **wear**y,
  Went to **sleep** while others **rowed**.
So He **did**n't know when **trou**ble
  Made them **wish** they could be **towed**.

Clouds were **black** and threatened **thun**der.
  Wind was **fierce;** waves blew **high**.
Panic **set** their hands to **bail**ing
  While they **feared** they just might **die**.

"Jesus! **Jesus**! We're in **trou**ble.
    Don't you **care**? We're going **down**."
The dis**ci**ples shook Him **fierce**ly
    As the **rains** came pelting **down**.

Jesus **woke** and stood be**fore** them.
    Turned to **face** the stormy **seas**.
Raised His **hands** as if to **sig**nal
    That the **storm** was soon to **freeze**.

"Peace be **still**!" His voice was **thun**derous.
    Like a **child** in stern re**buke**.
Wind and **waves** abruptly **si**lenced.
    Met their **match** with just a **look**.

In the **calm** He asked His **fol**lowers,
    "Have you no **faith**? Were you a**fraid**?"
And they **whis**pered, "Who is **with** us?
    He just **spoke** and winds o**beyed**!"

In the **gen**tle ride to **shore**line,
    Peaceful **out**side; inside **too**!
They were **full** of awe and **won**der
    At the **storm** He'd brought them **through**.

Life is **full** of stormy **path**ways.
    Wind and **waves** can threaten **too**.
Christ who **stilled** the stormy **wa**ters
    Stands to **still** a storm for **you**.

Performance Idea:

Share this piece as a rhythm story. Use an adult leader or pick an expressive reader from your group of actors.

All face the audience, clap time, and share the story by echoing the narrator. No costumes are necessary. If desired, you can replace clapping with rhythmic motions and steps.

Why not let the audience join in the echo response too?

7

A LOST COIN

(Luke 15:8-10)

See previous instructions.

Jesus told a **story**.
   I **want** to hear it **too**.
About a woman **los**ing
   A **coin** that sparkled **new**.

She **looked** and looked all **over**.
   She **searched** in every **place**.
She **thought** she'd never **find** it.
   A **frown** crept on her **face**.

She **cleaned** in every **corn**er
   When **sud**denly she **saw** it:
A **tiny** glint of **gleam**ing gold
   From **und**erneath the **car**pet.

"I **found** it. Oh, I **found** it!"
   She **cupped** it in her **hands**.
And **with** her newfound **trea**sure,
   She **raced** to tell her **friends**.

There **is** no greater **vict'**ry!
   There **is** no greater **prize**!
When **any** loser finds his **lost**,
   A **light** glows in his **eyes**.

The **light** of hope will **al**ways burn
   When **lost** things are a**round**.
And **no** one ever **hopes** like God
   Until His lost is **found**.

Performance Idea:

Use a narrator as a storyteller. Select a child actor to recite "I want to hear it too." Storyteller becomes the woman looking for the coin. When she looks, children also look without moving around too much. For last two stanzas, children stand, face audience, and deliver final memorized lines.

8

FOLLOW! FOLLOW!

(Matthew 4:19; Mark 10:21; Luke 9:59-62)

This rhythm story takes four claps per line.

Follow! Follow! Jesus **calls**.
Let My **words** direct you **all**.
Never detour. Never **stray**.
Always **follow** in My **way**.

Follow! Follow! **You** can **win**
If you **let** Him **have** your **sin**.
He will **save** you. **Then**, you'll **see**
How much **fun** your **life** will **be**.

Follow! Follow! Jesus **needs**
You and **me** to **plant** His **seeds**.
Can we **plant** them? **Do** we **dare**?
Can we **show** our **Lord** we **care**?

Follow! Follow! **Don't** just **sit**
When the **others** **want** to **quit**.
You can **finish**, **win** the **race**.
All you **do** is **keep** His **pace**.

Follow! Follow! **Don't** miss **out**.
This is **what** life's **all** a**bout**.
Follow Jesus **to** the **end**.
Let Him **be** your **very** best **Friend**!

Performance Idea:

Divide your acting group into five groups, one group for each stanza. Challenge the groups to come up with meaningful actions. Start with only the first stanza group onstage. Groups enter to deliver their stanza and stay. Delivery should be energetic and animated. Clapping will sustain consistent rhythm.

9

LEGION

(Mark 5:1-20)

For this rhythm story the leader speaks the first and last line. Everyone else repeats the words in italics. Clap on boldface. Practice the first stanza as an example.

Instruct the group that they will repeat the last word or phrase of your line twice and then repeat the whole line.

End the last clap of a stanza forcefully. Pause, as if to break the rhythm, and then restart it again for the next stanza.

Have you **ev**er heard of **Legion?**
Legion? Legion?
*Have you **ev**er heard of **Legion?***
Legion **who**?

He was **liv**ing in a **dead** place,
*A **dead** place, a **dead** place.*
*He was **liv**ing in a **dead** place.*
They **call** it a **tomb**.

He was **run**ning like a **man**iac,
*A **man**iac, a **man**iac.*
*He was **run**ning like a **man**iac;*
Crazy as a **loon**.

He would **cry** and even **cut** himself,
***Cut** himself, **cut** himself.*
*He would **cry** and even **cut** himself.*
And it **did**n't even **hurt**.

Then, **Je**sus came a**long** one day,
*A**long** one day, a**long** one day.*
*Then, **Je**sus came a**long** one day.*
And **Leg**ion called His **name**.

67

"Jesus, Son of **God** Most High!
*God Most High! **God** Most High!*
*Jesus, Son of **God** Most High!*
What **do** You want from **me**?"

Jesus asked him, "**What's** your name?
*What's your name? **What's** your name?*"
*Jesus asked him, "**What's** your name?"*
"**Me**? They call me **Le**gion.

"A **thou**sand demons **live** in me!
*Live in me! **live** in me!*
*A **thou**sand demons **live** in me!*
But **please** don't let them **go**!

"**Send** them to that **herd** of pigs,
*Herd of pigs, **herd** of pigs.*
*Send them to that **herd** of pigs*
And **they'll** leave me a**lone**."

So **Je**sus told the **de**mons, "Go!
*Demons, go! **demons**, go!"*
*So **Je**sus told the **de**mons, "Go!*
Don't **make** this man your **home**."

They **rushed** into the **pigs** nearby,
*Pigs nearby, **pigs** nearby.*
*They **rushed** into the **pigs** nearby*
And **ran** right off the **cliff**.

Legion was a **brand**-new man,
*A **brand**-new man, a **brand**-new man.*
*Legion was a **brand**-new man*
For **Christ** had made him **clean**.

He **dressed** with clothes and **combed** his hair,
*Combed his hair, **combed** his hair.*
*He **dressed** with clothes and **combed** his hair*
And **asked** to follow **Christ**.

"Go **home** and tell them **what** I did,
*What I did, **what** I did.*
*Go **home** and tell them **what** I did*
You're **need**ed most at **home**."

And **Jesus** tells us **all** the same,
*All the same, **all** the same.*
*And **Jesus** tells us **all** the same.*
Go **home** and talk of **Christ**.

Performance Idea:

Select actors to play the parts of LEGION and JESUS.

Dress LEGION in torn rags with chains on hands (paper ones would be fine) with a long enough lead to allow him room to move.

JESUS may wear traditional biblical costume.

Pantomime all actions. If you choose, the two characters could speak their own lines. Let the chorus group still repeat the echo lines. When the demons leave LEGION, have the echo group follow imaginary demons into imaginary pigs that run off an imaginary cliff, while echo group covers eyes in surprise and disbelief.

At the end, LEGION can put on a clean shirt to represent his new person. With the last line, ask speaking group to point to audience.

10

THE SAND HOUSE

(Matthew 7:24-27; Luke 6:47-49)

Assign half the group to be hammers by hitting palm with clenched fist. Assign the other half to be saws by sliding edge of hand against the other palm and making a swishing noise.

Use these sounds to establish rhythm, instead of clapping. Use these same instructions for "The Rock House," which follows.

> **Get** out your **ham**mer! *(Hammers begin)*
> **Get** out your **saw**! *(Saws begin)*
> **We'll** build a **house**
> That **will** not **fall**.
>
> We **need** a foun**da**tion,
> **Some**thing quick to **lay**.
> I **want** to build this **house**
> In **less** than a **day**.
>
> **Get** me some **sand**.
> It's **eas**y to **find**.
> **Shov**el it and **spread** it.
> **Lev**el on a **line**.
>
> **Now** to the **buil**ding.
> **Care**ful with the **wood**.
> And **soon** we'll see a **house**
> Where **once** a forest **stood**.
>
> **Now** the building's **o**ver. *(Building sounds stop)*
> **Now** we move right **in**.
> **Let** it rain and **thun**der.
> **We'll** stay dry with**in**.
>
> But **wait**! I hear the **thun**der,
> And **ev**en though it's **night**,
> I **see** the rain in **splash**es.
> I **see** the flash of **light**.

The **floor** is shaking **wild**ly
And **sink**ing in the **land**.
The **house** I built is **fall**ing
And **I'm** on sinking **sand**. *(All clap.)*

Jesus told this **sto**ry *(Start hammer and saw sounds again)*
So that **all** of us would **think**.
A**bout** the life we're **build**ing
And **what** could make it **sink**.

Ins**tead** of building **hous**es
Up**on** some **sink**ing land
We **need** to build upon the **Rock**
That **won't** give way like **sand**.

Performance Idea:

Use a responding echo group who also make hammer and saw sounds as directed. Add thunder and rain sound effects on cue if desired.

When the house gives way, all actors could fall. Caution them to be ready to get up quickly, ready for the last two stanzas with hammer and saw sounds again.

On the last two lines, ask echo group to link arms with a closing show of strength.

11

THE ROCK HOUSE

(Matthew 7:24-27; Luke 6:47-49)

Use same instructions and Performance Ideas from "The Sand House."

Get out your **ham**mer! *(Hammers begin)*
   Get out your **saw**! *(Saws begin)*
Let's build a **house**
   That **will** not **fall**.

We'll **need** a good foun**da**tion,
   Something very **strong**.
Even though it's **cost**ly
   With **rock** you can't go **wrong**.

Haul it from the **moun**tain.
   Haul it from the **shore**.
Dig and lay it **lev**el.
   Then, **go** and get some **more**.

The **work** is hard and **heav**y.
   Some **think** it just a **waste**.
But **wait** until a **storm** arrives.
   They'll **wish** their house as **safe**.

Do you hear some **thun**der? *(Building sounds stop)*
   Is that rain I **see**?
Let's go in and **wait** it out.
   We're **safe** as safe can **be**.

It's **true** enough, when **storms** come
   Rock is what you **need**.
A **house** upon the **rock** will stand.
   It's a **mes**sage you should **heed**!

The **same** is true with **your** life
   He **tells** us one and **all**
Life **built** upon the Rock of **God**
   Will **never** ever **fall**.

APPENDIX A

Warm-up Exercises

These exercises can be used for any dramatic experience with children. Choose the one that best leads into the dramatic activity of the script. For example: "Animal Walk" is a good activity when the children need to act like animals. Adapt the exercises to fit the needs of the script and to enhance the focus of your rehearsal.

Animal Walk

Variation I

Place an animal sticker on a 3" x 5" card. Use animals like bear, duck, monkey, goat, etc. Make three to four of each animal card. Hand out a card to each individual and ask each participant to keep the animal a secret. Then, on cue, ask everyone to walk around the room without making a sound and act like the animal on the card. They are to find others who are acting like the animal they were assigned. It is an easy way to divide into groups for another activity.

Variation II

Prepare the cards as before but use a set of animals that can be easily identified by their sounds. (Example: lion, cat, duck, dog, etc.) Hand out the cards and ask them to walk and sound like the animal to find their group.

Variation III

Start this activity in small groups of no more than three. Make animal cards as above, this time using more difficult animals. (Example: elephant, giraffe, ostrich) Hand a card to each group. The group must then find a way to put their bodies together to represent the animal on the card. Ask each group to share their animal with the others. Results are fun to watch.

Charades

This familiar party game makes a wonderful warm-up activity, especially if you use characters, lines, or objects from your play. You can also develop character, emotion, and action cards to use on a regular basis.

Director Says

Use this game to introduce and review stage vocabulary. Gather the children on the stage or in a cleared space in your rehearsal room. Give stage directions such as "Take two steps downstage." Just as in Simon Says, the children are to follow only the statements you make preceded by "the director says . . ."

Finish This Line

Choose some key lines from the play. Give only part of the line and ask the group to "Finish this line." Actors who think they can must stand up and repeat the whole line. Have candy kisses to give to those who complete the line correctly. Take farther, if desired, by asking for where the actor stands to deliver the line, who the line is delivered to, etc.

Freeze Play

Have actors stand in a large circle. Have each actor choose an action or character from the play. It does not have to be the part they have been assigned. Instruct everyone to walk around the circle until you call "Freeze." Then, affirm good ideas. Continue playing by allowing actors to experiment with different ideas. Another variation is to introduce a what-if motivation that changes the actions and responses. Talk about the changes. You may also warn actors that you may call a Freeze Play at any moment. Use this technique when you need to fine-tune placement in group scenes.

Instant Puppet

For this activity, you need a handkerchief-sized piece of material, a sheet of newspaper to be wadded, and three rubber bands for each person who will make a puppet. Wad the paper into a ball around the index finger. Place the material square over the ball. Secure the first rubber band underneath the ball to identify a head. Secure the second and third rubber bands over material-covered thumb and second finger to make the puppet's hands. Add no facial expressions.

Direct your puppeteers through some exercises where they must make their puppet demonstrate an emotion such as happy, sad, angry, worried. They may also demonstrate actions: praying, saying good-bye, crying.

Watch the faces of your puppeteers as they do this. You will find their faces very expressive. This is a good exercise to focus on how the body communicates.

Machine

Part I

Cut out pictures of household machines from a catalog and paste them on 3" x 5" cards. (Example: popcorn popper, vacuum cleaner, toaster, lawnmower) Divide into groups of three to four. Hand out a card to each group. Tell the groups they are to use their bodies to make the machine. After giving a short time to practice, allow groups to share their machines with the whole group.

Part II

If using at a different rehearsal, give time for each group to practice their machine the way they shared it from the last rehearsal. Then, tell the groups to decide how their machine breaks down and what happens as a result. Does it slow down, speed up, work incorrectly, etc.

Next, ask the groups to decide what happens to the broken machine. Is it repaired, is it hopelessly broken, etc. Share comparisons between the parts of a machine and the different actors working together on a play.

Make a Face

Compose some one-line statements that evoke an emotional response and ask your group to "Make a face" to reflect the emotion. For example: "School's out!" "Your dog died." "Mom says you can't watch your favorite TV show."

Mirror

Actors pair up. Identify a leader and a follower. The leader uses his face, arms, and body while feet remain planted to one spot and the follower "mirrors" the activity. The idea is to accomplish such teamwork that it is difficult to determine who is leader and who is follower.

After a few minutes, reverse leader and follower. Encourage pair to discuss how to accomplish better unity.

Bring the exercise back when there are acting pairs who need to learn how to work together.

Name Tag

Suggest a symbol or group of symbols from the play. Ask children to draw or cut out one of the symbols and use as a name tag. Later, after parts have been assigned, give actors a chance to choose a symbol that best represents their character.

On the Spot

Have the children stand or sit in a circle. You begin by taking a place in the center of circle. Close your eyes and turn around a couple of times. Then, point to someone without knowing who it is. That person must quote a line from his part in the play. Then, that character takes a turn in the center. Continue the game until everyone has had a chance to give a line. No line may be repeated.

Pair Off

This is one way to introduce a kind of group pantomime and teamwork at the same time. Ask the group to pair off with the person on the right. If necessary, use one group of three. Then, suggest short, pantomime actions that require more than one person to complete. Select actions that relate to the play, if possible. Examples: playing on a see-saw, mending a net, moving a sofa. Be as concrete with the action and object involved as possible. Later, you can introduce more open-ended pantomimes where the children must define the object for themselves.

Pass It On

Sit in a circle with your group. Explain that you have an imaginary object to pass around. It can be anything from a butterfly trying to escape, an apple or a rose, or some object that is important to the play. Identify the object to the group. Everyone must take the imaginary object in their hands, examine it, do something with it, and "pass it on" without losing it.

Round-Robin Memorization

Sit in a circle. Without books or scripts, have actors quote lines, repeating them in sequence as fast as possible but not so fast that it becomes needlessly silly.

Tongue Twisters

Compile your favorite list of tongue twisters. The object of this exercise is improved articulation. Try handing out tongue twisters privately and give these children a chance to practice. Then, have them repeat the tongue twister for everyone. The catch is that the group must correctly identify each word in the twister. Get the children to bring in their favorite tongue twisters. This is an easy way to build your supply.

Word You Heard

This is similar to Make a Face except you only give one word for the group to respond to. For example: angry, excited, confused. Make sure to start with easy to identify emotions. Work toward less stereotyped ones such as: contented, frustrated. Variation 1: Start by ordering your words by opposites. Variation 2: Give a string of related emotions, like happy, excited, ecstatic. Talk about the ways to show differences.

APPENDIX B

Staging Positions for "You Can Choose"

Make a rehearsal cue card for each position listed below. Use them to help actors learn their positions for the sketch "You Can Choose" (see page 43). Keep the cue cards with an easy-to-see representative number even when there are more or less actors involved.

MASTER CHART

6	7	8	9	10
☹	☹	☹	☹	☹
1	2	3	4	5
☺	☺	☺	☺	☺

Position A

(Home Base)

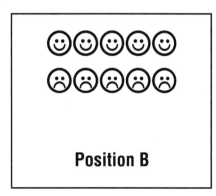

Position B

Position C

☺☺☺☺☺✝☺☺☺☺

Position D

☺☹☺☹☺☹☺☹☺☹

Position E

☺○☺○☺○☺○☺

Position F

☺☺☺☺☺☺☺☺☺